I Have A Name
A Prose Collection About Disorders

Creative Talents Unleashed

GENERAL INFORMATION

I Have A Name

By

Creative Talents Unleashed

1st Edition: 2017

This Publishing is protected under Copyright Law as a "Collection". All rights for all submissions are retained by the Individual Author and or Artist. No part of this publishing may be Reproduced, Transferred in any manner without the prior **WRITTEN CONSENT** of the "Material Owner" or its Representative Creative Talents Unleashed.

www.ctupublishinggroup.com

Publisher Information
1st Edition: Creative Talents Unleashed
info@ctupublishinggroup.com

This Collection is protected under U.S. and International Copyright laws

Copyright © 2017: Creative Talents Unleashed

ISBN-13: 978-1-945791-36-9 (Creative Talents Unleashed)
ISBN-10: 1-945791-36-5

Credits

Book Cover
Raja Williams

Creative Director
Brenda-Lee Ranta

Editors
Authors Responsible For Own Work

Preface
Brenda-Lee Ranta

Preface

I Have A Name

We live in a society whereby there is an astounding increase in what is known as 'the invisible disorders.' We may be living with one or more of them ourselves, or perhaps it could be our parent, our child, our grandchild or the person working at the desk beside us. These hidden, or not so hidden disorders are a part of our modern-day life, symptoms of hereditary, dietary, metabolic or chemical unbalances in the body – yet they exist and are very real for the person who lives daily with any of them.

There are many people silently suffering as a result. They are walking through life feeling lost, unsupported, misunderstood and alone; yet there is hope in acceptance and inclusion. There is hope when we give these disorders a voice, a name, a face and a place in society. The collection within these pages are voices, names and faces; the accounts of real people by real people. They either live with a disorder or have been deeply touched by knowing someone who does.

It is with my profound thanks to all the contributors, for opening themselves up, with the willingness to share these experiences with the world. *"You Have a Name."*

Brenda-Lee Ranta

Table of Contents

Preface   v

Depression

Untitled *Lynn Beringer*	2
Without Dreams *Nicole Metts*	3
The Fog *Steve Lay*	4
Mind's Prey *Markus Fleischmann*	5
Clarity *Karla Botha*	7
Darkness *Dawn Van Leeuwen*	8
Mistress *Maggie Mae*	9
Half Full Glass *Shelly Buttenhoff Miller*	10
Depression *Don Beukes*	11
Baby Steps *William Wright, Jr.*	12

Table of Contents

Athenaeum of the Forsaken *Ken Allan Dronsfield*	13
Destination Hope *Amanda J. Evans*	14
Strip Me of Ambition *Cory Costantino*	15
It Takes Over Me *A.M. Torres*	16
Hopeless *Markus Fleischmann*	17
A Thwarted Undoing *C.J. Clark*	19
Job of Living *Shelly Buttenhoff Miller*	20
Black Dog *Steve Lay*	21
Mercy Killing *William Wright, Jr.*	22
Stretching Back *Cory Costantino*	23
DEPRESSION *Krista Vowell Clark*	24
Depression Confession *Don Beukes*	25

Table of Contents

The Fight *Sagar Singh*	26
Back Again the Wall *Shelly Buttenhoff Miller*	27
Voices *Kelly Jadon*	28
Crumpled *Justin R. Hart*	29
House of Clay *Karla Botha*	30
Pretend *C.J. Clark*	31
Two Poles *Markus Fleischmann*	32
I'm Not There *Barbara Suen*	33

Anxiety

The Box *Lynne Reeder*	36
I Don't Have Anxiety *Jessica Trudel*	37

Table of Contents

Release Grip *Christa Frazee*	38
It's Real *Dawn Van Leeuwen*	40
A Silent Fight *Renee Kline*	41
Selling the Drama *Jez Rico Cuenta*	43
Madness *Amanda J. Evans*	44
These Four Walls *Linsey Matthews*	45
Anxiety *Justin R. Hart*	46
Deafening Silence *Nicole Metts*	47
Screwed Up *Lynn White*	48
Quietly Dead *Sandra Orellana*	50
Butterflies *Alayna Lauver*	51
The Intruders *Carolyn Gutierrez-Abanggan*	52

Table of Contents

Sleepless   54
Ann Christine Tabaka

Beside Myself   55
Justin R. Hart

White Noise   56
Hugh Dysart

When Demons Play   57
Kathy-Lynn Cross

Obsessive ~ Compulsive Disorder

The Precipice   60
Kelly Jadon

One Life to Live   61
Tara Phillips

Five   62
Sandra Kramer

The Paper Guy   63
Brenda-Lee Ranta

Naysayers   64
Lilly Moore

Combustion   65
Ann Christine Tabaka

No One Wants to be the Joke   66
Linda M. Crate

Table of Contents

Autism ~ Asperger's Syndrome

Convey *A.M. Torres*	68
Autistic Alone *Jyotirmaya Thakur*	69
Hold My Hand Grampa *Hugh Dysart*	70
Opposing Mirrors *Mark Andrew Heathcote*	71
Savant *Susan E. Birch*	72
On Autism *Fatima Afshan*	73
Judo Suits *Mark Andrew Heathcote*	74
The Question *Brenda-Lee Ranta*	76

Attention Deficit Hyperactivity Disorder

Undiagnosed Disorder *Don Beukes*	78

Table of Contents

The Misfits Understand   79
Leigha Beltrame Markon

What is Normal?   80
Veronique Ginglo-Robert

Never on the Good Side   81
D.B. Hall

The Alphabet Kid   83
Lynne Reeder

ADHD   85
Don Beukes

I Fell in Love with ADHD   86
Veronique Ginglo-Robert

Schizophrenia

Seroquel Slumber   88
Christa Frazee

Lunatic Shuffle   89
Ken Allan Dronsfield

The Voices   91
Hugh Dysart

Mysylum   93
Billy Charles Root

Table of Contents

Schizophrenics *Mark Andrew Heathcote*	95
Head People *Brenda-Lee Ranta*	96
Crude and Hollow *William Wright, Jr.*	98
North of Reality *C.J. Clark*	99
Downward Spiral *Carolyn Gutierrez-Abanggan*	100

Bipolar ~ Personality Disorder

Bubbles of Emotion *Lilly Moore*	104
I Have a Name (slipping away) *Dawn Van Leeuwen*	106
Insanity *Billy Charles Root*	107
Bipolar Mind *Kelly Klein*	109
Set Me Free *D. B. Hall*	111

Table of Contents

The Park of Life *Jackie Chou*	112
Self-Medicated *Lynne Reeder*	113
White Noise (scream out) *Renee Kline*	114
Manic Kiss *Christa Frazee*	115
Psycho *Mahinour Tawfik*	116
With Love from Bi-Polar in Alaska *Lyne Beringer*	117
I Cannot Let the Nightmares Win *Linda M. Crate*	118
Blissfully Waiting for Lithium's Last Kiss *Ken Allan Dronsfield*	119
On Level Ground *John Walker*	120
It's Where I Hide *Kathy-Lynn Cross*	121
I Have a Name (It Could be Anyone's) *Lyne Beringer*	122

Table of Contents

Epilogue

The Starving Artist Fund   126

CTU Connections   128

I Have A Name

Depression

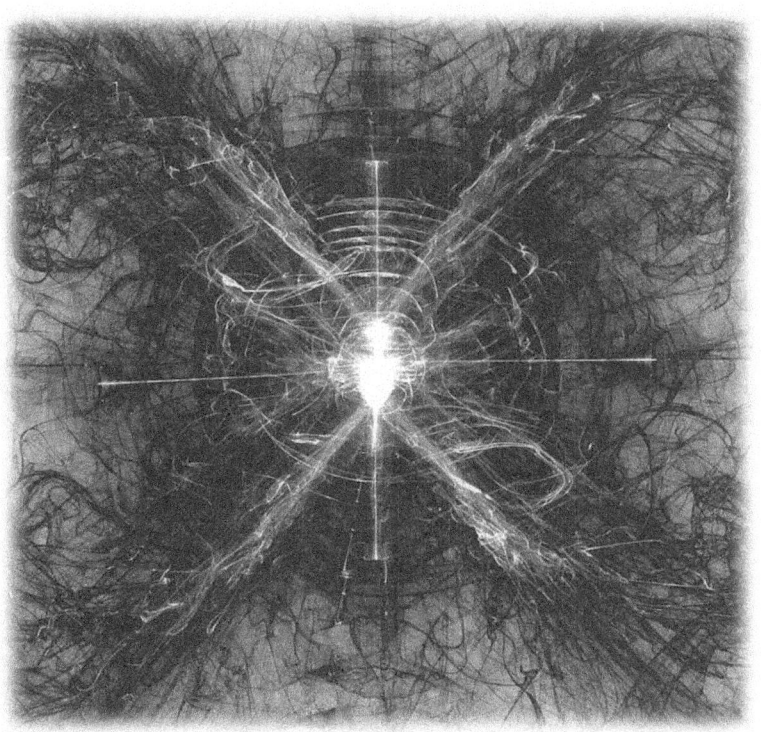

Untitled

I waited until I withered away
Then winter came....
Bringing the wind with it
Now… I am the storm that rages……

Lyne Beringer

Without Dreams

The sunshine's in an endless night, allowing no sleep.
The birds do not sing.
The stars have lost their luster, without dreams.
Bodies curl and intertwine with nothing to say.
Oceans tide high, while insects swarm replacing clouds.
Flowers curl inside their selves; hiding pedals beneath their leaves.
Roots of trees climb their own branches,
As fish retreat, farther into the abyss.
All of fur and feather join the sea,
Fully masked in silk; I lay upon a bed of nails
Unable to imagine a white picket fence for counting sheep.

Nicole Metts

The Fog

The fog is rising over the mountain tops,
Blocking out all the morning sun,
Makes it sometimes hard to see,
The true colours of everyone.

The fog is right in front of my eyes,
It's blocking out the sun beginning to rise,
Where is the horizon and the shore,
I can't see my feet on the floor.

The fog is rising as the boat floats,
After rain clouds have started pouring down,
Someday there will be a rainbow,
From tears where we nearly drowned.

Feels like someone got inside my head,
Turned it around and around,
Put one foot in front of the other,
When my head will clear now.

Steve Lay

I Have A Name

Mind's Prey

I can feel it
Crawling in my head
Like a spider in a can
Weaving a web
A trap
Capturing the light
I once had
I can sense it
In my veins
Like Vernon
Slowly driving me insane
Regret
Shame
Self-blame
My thoughts are no longer
The same
It sneaks in my dreams
Silently screams
My thoughts turned
Into delusions
Emotions become illusions
I can feel it
Slithering inside
My sanity has no place
Left to hide
It gnaws
Scratches and bites
Day and night
I'm afraid to speak
For in my words it creeps
Tortures me as I sleep
It won't stop until
I bleed

I Have A Name

Cut deep meaning to
Set it free
I can feel it
Inside of me
My soul cries
It pleads
I can feel it
See it....

Markus Fleischmann

Clarity

Take a pause for an emotional twist,
Fake a smile, clench the teeth – make a fist,
False-felt provocative prophecy,
Inevitably failed a never made destiny.

So many words, I drown in decay,
Too many demons, I cannot slay,
Apathy turns pity, spent in shattered reflective sea,
Sinner boy turns sinner man and remembers me.

This beauty be self-made socialism, turned hypocrisy,
Yet demons do not turn, but simply adhere to hierarchy,
Trust is not questioned in here bench marked court,
Rather how a diamond could dare to think a charcoal thought.

Can daughter wind cry to a dying heart?
Without mother-earth to tell her fluid sounds apart?
Too many times we retreat in un-relying sympathy,
A hundred ways to float past clarity.

Karla Botha

Darkness

The absence of light.
I have no light, no laughter, no joy.
Only darkness.
Heavy, oppressive darkness.
It seems endless, this dark place.
Yet there is comfort here, at times.
Like the arms of a lover protecting me from the world.
Devoid of feeling, a shield of numbness,
but not life.
I want to live, to laugh, to love.
Teach me.

Dawn Van Leeuwen

Mistress

Depression is
A vicious mistress
She lulls you
Into a quiet sleep
To awaken you
With nightmares
Of pain
The mistress
Of sadness
She pulls and pushes
Until the abyss
Is full of ghosts
Of loss and failure
No light
No love

Depression is
A vicious mistress
Do not accept
Her gifts
Solitude and tears
Do not listen
To her negative whispers
No matter what
She chatters
You are beautiful
You do have worth
You are loved

Maggie Mae

Half Full Glass

The glass is
Never half full
Nor is it half empty
In fact, the glass
Is completely empty
I have no more to give
Depression and anxiety
Have set in
Keeping my glass empty
Hope is lost
I am lost

Even so I keep
Working my program,
Taking medications,
Talking to my therapist,
Going to appointments,
Attending classes and groups and
Spending time with friends

Slowly the condensation
Builds in the glass as it
Becomes half empty
I know
Without a doubt
If I keep at it
My glass will become
Half full
As my life is becoming
One worth living

Shelly Buttenhoff Miller

Depression

Forced to face my inner demons
I blame myself for my elected
negligence in understanding my
historic tsunamis of erratic masked
emotions – I guess it began with
childhood feelings of worthlessness
suppressing floods of negative feelings
as I conveniently preferred listening
to my own two-way mutterings in my
exclusive private head space trying
not to feel like a lost head case.

I used to verbalize my thoughts and
frustrations deep within my mental
chambers – My daily stage performance
since primary school faking my smile
whilst drowning within – The result

Don Beukes

Baby Steps

I am staggering
Below, the broad strides of giants
All chemically safe and sound

I am finally staggering for euphoria's reach
In a swell of despair
That coats me in rot

A shudder from within
Sends the cold ground hurtling
Nearer and nearer
As the cries of the heard
All recede into dust

And I'm reduced to a crawl
Gathering steam
For the forward lunge of defiance

William Wright, Jr.

Athenaeum of the Forsaken

I am simply too sad to be awake,
drowning in tears of blood and fate.
It's hard to take even one more breath,
much too ambivalent to wallow in death.
Deviant smiles devoid of simple clownery
carnivals of joyous splendor are upon me.
Colored clothes burn greedily in the fire pit.
black hooded smocks calm my Gothic spirit.
Pastures await those of incessant grazing,
perhaps I'm not lonely just a bit of the crazy
spellbound by the dark egotistical minds,
waking is precious when in pandiculation.
Cadence of the heart rarely skips a beat,
our world slows to many of ethereal piety.
Chameleonic jealousy can finally take a seat
awaken my friend, is this not but a dream?

Ken Allan Dronsfield

Destination Hope

The road leads nowhere
Dusty and desolate,
filled with chipped concrete and rocks,
abandoned like my thoughts

My road
Misshapen, isolated,
A padded room, no escape.

I look into the distance
black and eerie,
like Sulphur covered remnants
my house burned to the ground

Silence, no happy chirping
to sing me on my way
No colour in the scorched fields
My path lifeless and barren

I struggle forward
one step at a time
fragmented memories torment
this fragile mind

Yearning for the yellow brick pathway
golden sunlight, sounds of life
A powerful wizard to send me home

But this is my road
my tormented path
isolation of a mind
struggling to break free

Amanda J. Evans

Strip Me of Ambition

I want to not be tired
like I always am
and when I am not tired
I want to be restful
like my life is ahead of me,

but strip me of ambition
so, I might rest with the knowledge
that I will not be tired again
by the next stretch wearing me down
falling short enough to matter
and close enough to keep me going,

tired, tired, and tired some more.
thoughts make me tired;
thinking of what I want
what I know can be done
what the world could become
if I weren't so tired

If I could forget what I've been through,
if my body didn't know the pattern by now
I might overcome
but I will succumb
and nothing will be done
except I will somehow muster the will
to care enough
about an effort that I know
will tire me too much

Cory Costantino

It Takes Over Me

How they judge me
Not feeling my strife,
The sadness I feel
My longings to die.
They tell me to fight
I could if I want,
I've let it come in
Allowed it to win.
That is not so,
My days pass so slow,
I didn't ask for this
This feeling is hell.

Not that they see
They view me as weak,
A quitter in life
Depression so bleak.
If only I could
I've struggled to fight,
I struggle to eat
It takes over me.
It drains my soul
Depression frosts me,
The die has been cast
How lonely I be.
With no support
They can't understand
It robs me of strength
It takes over me.

A.M. Torres

Hopeless

Shadows on silent walls
Play out a frightening scene
Murder of my wishing dreams
Lonely does my mind whisper
To the lull
Loss of ambiance of night
My thoughts tease with trickery
Illusionary images of hope
Cast on its reflective surface
Waiting...
Waiting for ripples to once again
Distort the image into the reality
A once dreamt life
Torn with lies
A once happy heart
Lost.
Lost to the hush of night
With only silhouettes of what could
Will never be dancing on the wall's
Empty cold canvas
Dreams once cherished
Once pleasant to my soul
Find hurt evermore
Night after night
In my sleepless mind
My fear upon waking
Is not the day holding hope?
It is of my hope
My dream
My wish
Lost in the silence
Stolen by its absence
Only its silhouettes

I Have A Name

On my darkened wall
Remain dancing

Markus Fleischmann

A Thwarted Undoing

She had slumped over
Into her new self
Feeling the strangeness of it
Grip her
Like trying on a new coat
Frozen from hanging
In corridors
Of icy drafts
Her new voice had no volume
It was thin and betrayed her
Forming words
She never intended
Her feet shuffled
In empty slippers
Moving in no
Particular direction
She clung to her husband
A kind stranger now
Someone she may
Have once known
It was all she'd truly wanted
Folds of soft kindness
Cascading around her
Securing her in warmth
Allowing her to embrace
The peace of long slumber
Until she could find
Some other way out.

C. J. Clark

Job of Living

It comes
Creeping in
So subtle sometimes
Suddenly struck
Like lightening
Flashes of dark thoughts
Bring sorrowing emotions
Settling in
Taking over my
Very heart and body
Lethargy
Hopelessness
Helplessness
As to what my
Next step should be

How impossible it is
To get back to the
Job of living

Shelly Buttenhoff Miller

Black Dog

Black dog jumping up and down,
chasing its tail all around,
Keeps playing but it comes with a bite,
throw its toy to it, comes with a fight
Can't just leave it at home,
so that is free to roam,
give a dog a bone,
chasing after you.

Walking my way home tonight,
looked up yonder the sky was bright,
Suddenly like a Tidal wave,
the bright was gone and it gave way
Moon of blood, pool of black,
ten ton weight I felt on my back,
weighing me down, I felt like I could drown.

Black dog running through the fog,
searching for the light,
Walking in a direction looking for a light,
walking in a direction looking for the bright
Gives new meaning to the feeling,
lights are on who is at home.
Black dog hanging around your neck
Black dog not wagging its tail on closer inspect.

Steve Lay

Mercy Killing

I've never had the stomach
to send this life crashing down
all around me, in a fit of distress

Eternity
pleads, in the dead of night
but I've never had the heart
to return its bitter-cold glare

The will is with me in brief
when I'm swarmed by the hateful past
When I've dwelt too long
in this shell of myself

William Wright, Jr.

Stretching Back

Stretching across a mountain of moments,
a compacted heap of wrappers and notes
once held or recorded the vast signals of a life
drilling through time I see what I have felt:
repeating patterns, spent layers of feeling compressed
finally squeezing out the air in between
where I try to insert subconsciously,
one more gasp, always one more gasp
of air that is not there, and make it seem it is the present,
a moment renewed, on news not new, and I wake up
to see layers of feeling already had and repeated
that I wouldn't feel again if I could stop and look
at the mountain of moments, I've already been
settling like bands in the soil marking
how often the ground shifted under my feet
but I stare so hard all I see is that moment
entombed in a layer,
and all I think is what is written on that scrap of paper,
and I forget where I am, then becomes now, again and
again...

Cory Costantino

I Have A Name

DEPRESSION

Despicable defiant deranged demoralized diabolical darkness

Excessive emotional eccentric earthshaking euphoric exhaustion

Passionate polyunsaturated painstaking pathetic powerless pandemonium

Rambunctious radioactive rattle-brained repetitive raging renegade

Extravagant enthusiastic elaborately exposed envious effervescence

Scintillating sarcastic smoldering sculpturesquely Sobering subconscious

Secret secluded semi-abstract shattered sensationalistic silence

Inarticulate illustrious intoxicating illuminated idiotic insanity

Obnoxious overabundant offbeat orphaned offensive obstruction

Nasty nauseating notorious narcissistic neurological nightmare

Krista Vowell Clark

Depression Confession

Depression
of early childhood bullying, my
genetic confusion maybe even a
necessary illusion –

Certainly, suffering emotional abuse from
a young age prevented to show emotion
or not conforming to the rules of a culture or
nation even a notion – A dismissal of emotions
I should have understood and recognized the
triggers, I have had my share of the loss of
loved ones – A mother, father, sisters, brothers,
uncles and aunts – A family tree too intricate
to explore, yet I admit their passing remains my
emotional sting – I should have walked away from
my profession the moment I experienced work place
oppression even institutionalized racism delivered in a
decade of foreign cynicism – My denial of my deepening
depression resulting in difficulties to work, sleep or eat,
sinking further in dream state alleys of woe drowning in my
sorrow fearing each tomorrow.

I'm better now – Somehow walking away from it all and
breaking the social mold has rejuvenated me healed me
renewed me liberated me from my emotional sarcophagus –
My deepening abyss as I leave you with this – My
depression confession...

Don Beukes

The fight

These voices in my head have gotten louder lately,
if only I had the courage to pull the trigger,
it soothes me,
the cold metal kissing my forehead,
My fingers sensing the power they crave,
the power to finally end this suffering.
The voices screaming to do it, end the pain;
I can feel the gunpowder as I inhale deeply,
but in between the noises, there's a whisper,
whisper that finds its way through the crowded streets of my mind,
All it says is, 'it gets better.'
and for just one more day,
I find the strength to keep the gun down.

Sagar Singh

Back Against the Wall

Back against the wall
Tears gliding down her face
Holding back sobs
Not enough tissues
There's never enough
Long, long day
Long, long life
She's so weary
Despair covers her like the fog
Shrouds the deadly waterfall ahead

Shelly Buttenhoff Miller

Voices

voices echo
repeating
themselves
redundant
memories
impressions
over and over
never ending
never muted
but covered
by surf's roar
upon beach's sand
where i lie
face covered
attempting to ignore
trying to understand
the torment
never knowing
it was
a major depression

Kelly Jadon

Crumpled

Any paper
of a passionate page
that bends
the words so far
they finally fold to
the side of the others
will
cause an effect
crease its crumpled core
balling
and then straightening up
trying
to forever unfold
without one
being
completely
open again

Justin R. Hart

House of Clay

Depression is repression,
You make me open up my doors,
A beautiful conflict presides inside,
A whirlwind that's now yours.

So sorry to say,
Contradicting issues mucks up my mind,
Anger blinded crusade,
For innocence, I'll never find.

Don't let me fall,
Into me,
Don't let me fail,
My own damned legacy.

A demon keeps glancing through the cracks,
My soul exposed to the other side,
A freak-train went through town,
You figured you'd catch a ride.

Search inside the dust window bay,
And look upon what you will find,
Draw the curtain crooked boy,
Step inside an artist's mind.

Karla Botha

Pretend

After long, hot days
Of careful breathing
Heaven waited
In the white light
Of believing
The eyes of joy
Would soon shut tight
Around soft wing beats
Of silence in flight,
Still, the earth
Would hold me here
Without a friend
My only comfort
This world of Pretend.

C. J. Clark

Two Poles

Sometimes I'm crying
No reason at all
Sometimes I'm drowning
Of the tears that fall
Sometimes I'm falling
With knees on the ground
Sometimes I'm up
Sometimes I'm down
Sometimes I'm further
Than I'd like to be
Simply existing
Just being me
I have no crown
No glory in me
It's not my story
Not what I see
Sometimes there is doubt
Pain deep inside
A darkness I fight
Within myself I hide
But sometimes
There's release
Those sometimes
When I'm not praying
On my knees
When I'm not shedding tears
When I conquered my fears
Sometimes is just that
A beautiful sometimes
Living in my head

Markus Fleischmann

I'm Not There

Once again, I'm supposed to be somewhere.
I am missing.
Somewhere, alone instead.
This is what I do.
This is what I have done.
I'm simply not there.

They don't expect me anymore,
To show up.
I am silent in feeling,
out of excuses,
and none are needed, you see?

I sit here on a beautiful summer day,
no longer wondering why
the calls become fewer,
the visits obsolete
How I love you,
but, showing up is part of that deal,
I know.

"Acceptance" is hard for loved ones.
They don't know
That "Solitude" is my best friend.
Solitude is my worst enemy.
I'm somewhere in the middle,
where no choice is still a choice.

No, I'm not there again.
"I'm sorry" become hollow after a while.
Will those be my last words?

Yes, I am missing.

I Have A Name

Missing, and missing out.
My only thought is
"How or if?"
I will ever be

"missed"

Barbara Suen

Anxiety

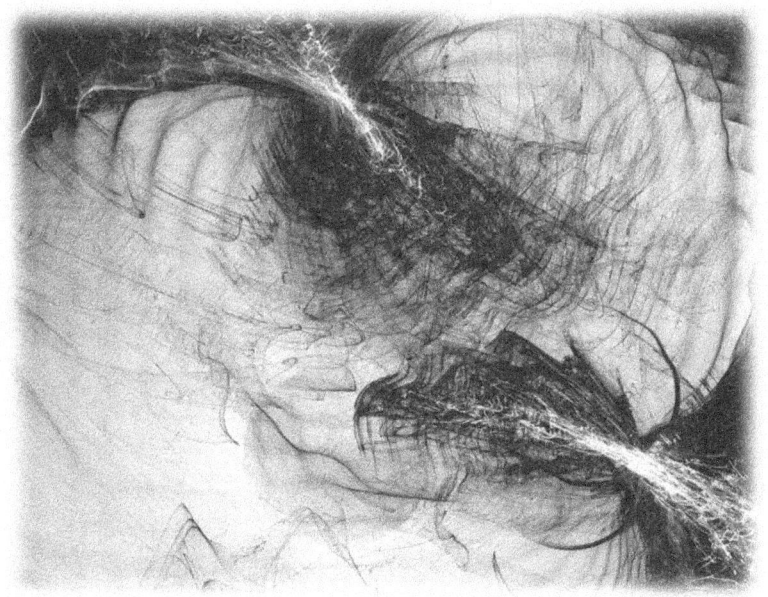

The Box

Black box
Cancer of the mind
Not so unlike the kind
That eats away at
My grandmother's insides--
My thoughts attacking
Then retracting
The way her own cells
Turn against themselves.
The battle within
Become tiresome
And heavy.
The black box now
Expanding
And whole.
I radiate cures for others
While my own heart
Metastasizes
And criticizes
Itself to the core.
I'll never be rid of
This malignancy,
This inconsistency
Of worth.
Black dark sanity
Gone cancerous
Since birth.

Lynne Reeder

I Don't Have Anxiety

I don't have anxiety
I have moments when
I don't have propriety
When I don't know who
is my proprietary
I have concerns about whom
will live my life while
I'm lying flat on the floor
I have unexpected reactions
to the slightest shifts
the lightest touches
I have hours when the tears
won't stop
I have racing thoughts
replaying words
long dead or yet unsaid
I have caffeine shakes
without the coffee
and exhaustion
without the effort
I don't have anxiety
Anxiety has me

Jessica Trudel

Release Grip

Agonized for centuries by the
Cruelty of my own mind.
The facts are past tense….
The experiences long-expired...
And yet, my brain refuses to
Release grip or even begin
The starting to forget...

Fretting, petting demons…
Neglecting the now as I
Skim over worn volumes...
Pacing within the vaults
Of every yesterday...
How truly humiliating.
To be left behind…
Excluded from your
Own life…

Others progress and
Mend their messes,
While I keep
Re-reading
Old remains…
Only so I can
Re-gather and
Re-gather and
Reevaluate again.

Viscous,
Persistent cycles…
Ugly, insistent modes
Of half-survival.

I Have A Name

Bring back the
Ease of laughter!!!
Oh, God~
Bring back the joy and hope...
Replace my pride & anxiety
With calm intentions and
Resuscitating light,
Soulfully administered.

Christa Frazee

It's Real

A tsunami raging toward me, engulfing me.
I'm going to die.
I have to leave.
Get up, just get up, get out!
I can't feel my legs.

Can't they see I'm drowning.
Someone help me.
Oh God, Please, someone save me.

No one is going to save me,
They can't see the tempest raging inside me.
I am alone.
Alone to find the surface, step onto dry land.
I can make it.
Get up.
Get out.
Relief!

Dawn Van Leeuwen

A Silent Fight

This young man standing there
with his aging face and thinning hair
Dark circles and black eyes
drink in hand, he sighs

Do you stop and wonder why?

He must be strung out you say
And you turn and look the other way
Born in a bad home, lives in poverty
Fell in with drink and drug, not an oddity

Now let me ask you this, would you still have him condemned
If he was your father, brother, son or friend?
Would you still your assail
If you knew his tale?

He was just a boy when he left
You could call it theft
His innocence shattered
But none of that mattered
He returned a man
Someone with a plan

Then it started many months ago
It wasn't as it seemed though
He wrestles with the night
He keeps his eyes open to block the sight
Nightmares keep the dreams away
demons rule here and they want to play

I Have A Name

The abyss threatens to swallow him whole
one bite at a time to claim his soul

He cries out in the dark answering the call
silently he carries it all

Guilt and fear with all that it implies
bound by secrets and lies
Pain and misery took hold
you'll get over it he was told
To him it just wasn't clear
how could his family still love him sincere?

He doesn't have it right
all love him through his plight
One day soon the nightmares subside
the healing begins inside

The story doesn't end here, a message to heed
everyone has their tale, we just need
Compassion, empathy and understanding
together we should be standing
United and not so assuming
after all we are all just human

Renee Kline

Selling the Drama

Howls of indignation shattered the night
Lamentations are on its heights
Agitation is written in the skies
More commotion raises tonight.

Wicked smile perilous mind
Inflicted feelings, sinners hand
Mournful hours bleeding inside
Destruction is what left behind

Granted with tears and grievances
Completely stir up with pure sadness
Wretched moments, such loneliness
Slowly devours my own goodness.

Now it's the time for awakening
The death is near the horrible scene
No doubt to disrupt my apathy
And I'm ready to face this tragedy.

Jez Rico Cuenta

Madness

The haunted voices
Stirring in my mind
Evil demons vying for my attention
Scrambling to the surface
Clawing, scratching, pulling
Bathing me in black
As I struggle to erase their existence

Trapped inside a glass tomb
Mind warped images
Scales covering
Whispers taunting
Screams of suffering

When will it end?
The incessant wailing
voices in my mind
Encouraging, plotting, teasing

I will not give in
I will not listen
Ears covered, mouth closed
Resisting the darkness
I beg to be set free

Amanda J. Evans

These Four Walls

Timid thoughts
Flittering about in my mind
Always escape me
As I run out of time
My life fleeing before me
Because I live in fear
Of all of the things
I once held dear
No pleasure or joy
As I hide inside
Nobody knowing
That I'm even alive
Day by day
It only gets worse
Living life
As if it were rehearsed
It's not me
It's who I've become
My insides hollow
Just like a drum
The once strong person
That stood so tall
Is now confined
By these four walls.

Linsey Matthews

Anxiety

First life
brought strength,
leading
to weakness,
to control
the fear,
which dealt
the frustration,
built up
the anger,
and caused
the attack
to break down
the defense,
and hide
the anxiety.
Fear
is the face
in the mirror…

Justin R. Hart

Deafening Silence

An empty space,
Filled of dust and darkness.
Indents in a carpet
Reveal ghostly possessions like me.
Untidiness brings slight relief.
No smell of lemon or bleach.
But silent screams,
uneasy panic,
Of misplaced shoes.
As if any second,
will not be my own.
The door will slam..

swallowing me whole.

Nicole Metts

Screwed Up

He bottled up his worries,
his fears,
and sealed them in
securely.
Put them inside a bottle firmly
corked.
Then he thought, suppose they grew

agitated
and, expanding with the heat
produced
forced the cork free from the bottle,
releasing all
those fears and anxieties to reoccupy
his being.

It was another worry
for him
to ponder and fret about.
He knew
a screw top bottle would have
been better,
would have kept them confined
more securely.

Too late
now though, to have that thought
done is done.
The best ideas are, always
too late.
Past has always passed.

And then,

I Have A Name

another thought came to him,
so timely.

Maybe he could he transfer them,
move them
to the bottle with the screw
fastening
and screw them up tight
without
letting them out of the bottle.
Without
letting them escape.
Without
giving them
freedom,
freedom
to invade
his soul,
his dreams,
his being
his reason
for being.

Such a risk
though.
Such a worry.

Lynn White

Quietly Dead

Her quietness with no
hope to fight
her being
has been forgotten
not awaken
to express her hatred
nowhere to go
she waits for nothing to happen
her world has become
what tormented her abuse
her gestures speak
one day
she will snap

Sandra Orellana

Butterflies

Have you ever felt the butterflies,
swarm inside your stomach
only to drown their wings with fear
like fingers to their wings
panic steals the magic dust
My mother told me to never steal
a butterfly's ability to fly
Only a selfish person would destroy
something so beautiful
So, tell me what happened
to the little girl that just let
the butterflies land gently on her cheek
Who felt the rush of excitement,
in just letting them soar
because now I feel butterflies
filling the gaps beneath my lungs
taking my breath away
but the happiness is laced with terror
and I rip the wings from the only
beautiful thing left inside of me

Alayna Lauver

The Intruders

I know their voices
skulking 'bout the labyrinth.
Convoluted lies;
whispering the cursed death wish-
a better choice than anguish.
They're ubiquitous.
Ravenous. Unforgiving.
Their sharp fangs seething
into my being. Marring,
reeking of mortal decay.

In my solitude
they clamor for Obeisance.
These heartless masters
have long fortified their walls
from foreboding invasion-
that's rightfully mine;
nevertheless, they managed
to take full control...
Savage, vicious puppeteers;
strings coiled around my vessel

My voice, an outcast;
left to its own devices.
Doomed to meander
aimlessly for days; seeking
refuge in these hostile worlds.
Consigned to endless
lambasting, denigration!
Where is my sanctum?
It is weakening, wilting.
Draining to the very dregs

I Have A Name

It is waiting for
Redemption. Restoration.
This voice to ascent.
Free me from the wrath of the
Monsters roaming in my head.

Carolyn Gutierrez-Abanggan

Sleepless

Cold dark nights
I cannot sleep
Minutes stretch into hours
I lay in bed and watch
As the moon slowly creeps across the sky
And the stars dance in and out
I think of you
Broken promises
Spilled wine carpet stain
Dying fire, shattered dish
All seems familiar yet strange
The clock ticks loudly
Echoing in my brain
I turn over once more
To stare at the wall
No end in sight
Then morning once again

Ann Christine Tabaka

Beside Myself

I lay beside
my sides and walls
forgotten futures
to behold.

I feel the weight
beside myself,
too often
a stranger untold.

Frozen by fear,
I'm depressed
from the anxiety
that will soon unfold.

Tearful man boy
beside myself,
at what new cost
will he be sold?

Yet, I wonder,
who is to blame
for splitting apart
from the mold?

Don't know who is
beside myself,
and the chill of it
is much too cold.

Justin R. Hart

White Noise

Let the white noise pass through you,
it's feeding time at the aural zoo
Let the crazy pass through you,
pay no mind to a lunatic's view

Ignore anxiety's heat and rage,
squirming in its filthy cage
Dismiss its pleas and persistence,
it's very existence

Slide the fear under your bed,
out of your life, out of your head
Unclaimed baggage, cast it out,
wasted grief you can live without

Anxiety, this slimy snake,
I've had more than I can take
Sweaty palms, racing mind,
panic starts, pressure climbs

Clouds in my field of vision,
fact, fiction, black condition
Day after day, smile, pretend,
pray to heaven this hell will end

Valium by volume
Impatient patients,
make good addicts

Hugh Dysart

When Demons Play

I hear the alarm and try to start my day,
Happy, bubbly, lips stretch into a half smile.
It feels fake, I come undone.
Doubt.
I hear the alarm and smash it,
Anger, dark, and venomous.
Seething internally, I want to scream.
Furious
I hear the alarm and cover my head,
Crying, emptiness, imploding from madness.
Praying for peace, searching for darkness.
Depression.
I hear the alarm and smack snooze,
Dread, fear, holding back salty tears.
Horrid thoughts plague my mind.
Anxiety
I hear the alarm.
Roll out of bed.
My breath is shaky.
As the demons play.

Kathy-Lynn Cross

I Have A Name

Obsessive Compulsive Disorder

The Precipice

her side woundless,
his wounded for transgression.
sin known and unknown,
passed from father to children,
giving them hope and many false starts,
which begin when the gun speaks
and shortly end when it repeats
drugs, like vitamins, a handful
thrown back with a coffee
chaser; he cannot care for himself

he cannot care for himself
that's OCD--the repetition of talk
which does not end, but causes
torment end to end, a perfect circle
hula-hooped in the head; an earworm
which plays over like a broken record,
like a return button - a return to what is
reality, what is real, what is inside the head,
mimicking itself, a silent mime unseen,
but deafly heard. its roar deafening
as Niagara's falls.
the precipice of the fall,
descent into psychotic symbiosis.

Kelly Jadon

I Have A Name

One Life to Live

Are you paralyzed by life - a struggle between acceptance and tolerance?
Afraid you will screw up your one and only life?
Write a saga of Obsessive Compulsive Disorder spelled out in binary code?
Zeros and Ones
As if the life-cycle only works in numbers; counting, calculations, and programming.
Impaired by lengthy overt rituals consumed by repetition and no solace.

Life's time clock ticks by unnoticed by the inner me.
Dreams and expectations unachieved.
Outside world passes me by unseen.
I only have one life to live.

Is there a soul behind the faceless body?
Mirrors fail to reflect how I feel;
afraid, disgusted, stuck in a state of disarray.
Lost in the deepest, darkest, disgruntled parts of my spirit alone and friendless.

Are there whispers in your ear of noise, chaos?
Intrusive visual, auditory or tactile sensations; mind play.
Was there ever a time more difficult than this?
Do you stare at yourself and wonder why, me, why OCD?
Why do I only have one life to live?

Tara Phillips

I Have A Name

Five

She is closing the windows, closing the curtains,
checking the latches and locks again to be certain
that all of the "bad guys" she fears
are out there when
she locks herself in here.

She is cutting her information from envelopes with scissors
reducing her name into bits
as she counts her security measures
as thin as each strip in a world
of more dangerous hackers
who bypass her snips, with their keyboards

She is counting the uneventful
hours with detailed precision.
one cannot go out at two
because three people on television
did something she noted four times.
but, by five they were going to prison.
She needs to hear this at six again.

One two three four five
Locks on the doors.
One two three four five
Ounces she pours
One two three four five
She counts them once more
because one must count something
when one counts for nothing.

Sandra Kramer

I Have A Name

The Paper Guy

*He was known in town as the 'paper guy,'
carried a bag full of newspapers, dropping
them off at counters of business locations*

Same route every day, without exception
Stopped in for coffee at the same restaurant,
walking the inside perimeter past the seated
patrons, circling three times exactly, before
sitting himself in the booth, facing the door;
never did he make eye contact with a soul

*The 'paper guy' got older, stopped delivering
papers; somehow finding a bike, which he
rode all summer, fall, winter and spring*

Same route every day, it had a basket that
he filled with odd articles; twine, sticks,
bottles, one glove, anything caught his eye
Mired in his routines, he would walk his
bike in snowstorms, the cold pinching his
face, always the same streets, same time

*We always wondered about his compulsions,
ritual circling of restaurants, obsession with
sameness of time and the sheer solemnity of it*

Brenda-Lee Ranta

Naysayers

To the mortal eye, curses would look a bit like dark colored light beams. In Room 2.68 of the Building of Fate, they appear out of nowhere. Sometimes, they come close enough to one of the many beige dummy puppets for them to blow on them. In those cases, the light beam splits-one half flies off to go about its usual business, and the other swirls and intertwines with the puppet's path.

If an outsider really were to look inside the Building of Fate, he would think Naysayers looked a lot like the other dummy puppets, only perhaps their bodies would show light specks of watercolor rather than be fully beige. If fact, they are nothing of the sort. Hardly anyone knows that Naysayers are one of the few forces that can counteract curses, forcing them away from the other puppets' paths.

Talia was one such Naysayer. Her torso was covered in soft blue swirls and her head was a mess of color. She was, perhaps, the most energetic of the lot, constantly knocking those dark-colored light beams away from the others, attacking once for blue, thrice for brown with an extra for more security and seven times for the horrible blacks.

When it got dark, the other puppets would whisper about her. "That girl is strange," they would say. "Why does she jump around and swivel her eyes like that?" they would wonder. "She's too scared to face reality," they would conclude. They didn't realize how much courage it took for her to ignore their whispers and to carry on deflecting curses. At least, that's what Talia thought.

Lilly Moore

Combustion

Deep within me there is a fire
A raging inferno that cannot be quenched
I feed it with images and words
It is fueled by my desire
A need to create
A need so great that it eats me whole
I am engulfed in the flames
Each trial more painful than the last
The fire consumes the oxygen
I can no longer breathe
There is no redemption
I must write to live

Ann Christine Tabaka

No One Wants to be the Joke

I don't want to be the aggravation or the laughing stock,
and I'm well aware of how neurotic I must seem;
always checking and rechecking to make sure the
door is locked or if I did something the right way three
times even when a part of my brain is telling me that this
isn't normal—
no one wants a mind full of whirring wires
that seem to never end one thought tumbling over another
in an unintelligent way until all one can focus on
is a failing economy of falling words that hit like
fallen rock and crash out of the cranium,
and no one wants to not be able to focus
because they're lost in another place which hurts
more than the one they're in; no one wants to drift
and be dragged into the sea forever forgotten
or have to arrange their food on the plate and
eat one thing at a time to be mocked by those
who're watching them—

no one likes being misunderstood.

Linda M. Crate

I Have A Name

Autism/Asperger's Syndrome

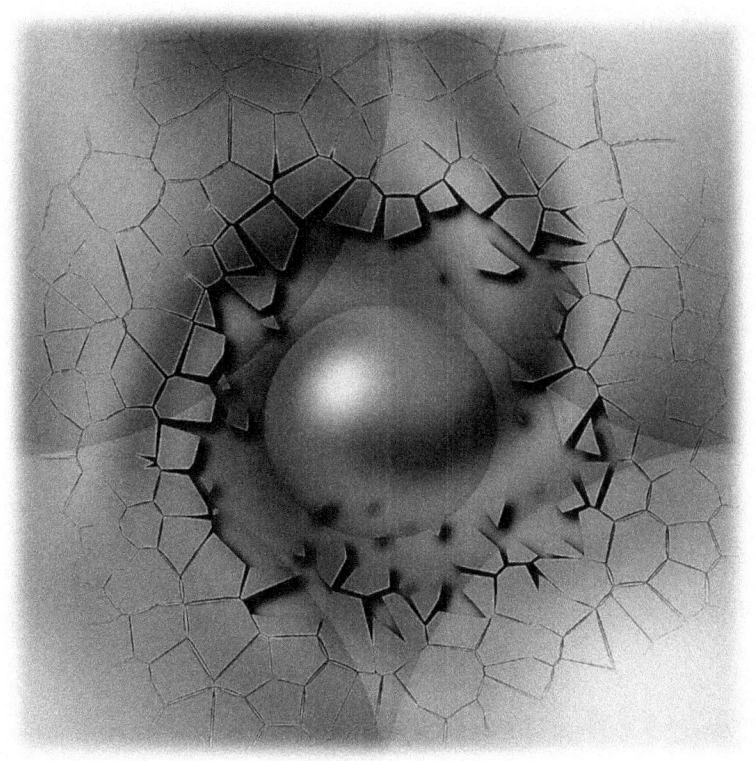

Convey

A scream, and long tears
His words come in spurts,
Convey, we try
We can make it work.
A baby in some ways
We fight to understand
A barrier it is
With words, yes, we can.
This longing is strong
To express more words
When questions arise
He longs to be heard.
It's not his fault
It's not what he asked
However, it's cast,
With patience, I have.
He's different, I know
He sees what I don't,
The world seen through him
He just wants to grow.
Somehow, we will
For he is much more
A special needs child
We must convey words.

A.M. Torres

Autistic Alone

I always thought I was a lotus in a pond,
the ugly duckling of a swan,
I had a life, a dream of my own
In my silence happy and withdrawn.
My parents cried when I sat alone,
Hours staring at a book or garden full blown,
Clapped in rain, opened windows in foul weather,
Repeated words of whisperings of others.
Howled like a dog or when thunders roared,
Threw tantrums for nothing but never respond.
I suffered from 'Autism' in medical term,
my parents fear just got confirmed.
Like any disease I could be treated,
a specialist consultant therapy needed.
'Echolalia'-is a term for language dysfunction,
I was confined to a room with designer decoration.
A school I joined with my special needs,
there were pure blossoms without any weeds.
Every cloud had a mysterious form,
who stole voices from the storm.
My day-dreams, fantasies new or old,
delusions, hallucinations turned to gold.

Jyotirmaya Thakur

Hold My Hand Grampa

Hold my hand Grampa,
hold it tight
Show me the way,
to where I'm
supposed to be
It will be alright
Hold my hand Grampa

Talk to me Grampa
Tell me how to say
"I love you"
Tell me everything
will be alright
It will be alright
Talk to me Grampa

Hold me tight Grampa
Never let me go
I feel your heart
crying for me
Don't cry Grampa,
everything will be alright
It will be alright

Hold my hand Grampa

Hugh Dysart

Opposing Mirrors

Morning shift; watching him launch himself
Watching him chasing "cabbage white" butterflies
in my mind's eye, it's a kind of carnival dance
one without any graceful feathery ranks
one whereby he's always out of step, out of tune
one in which both have danced back and forth,
through opposing mirrors and herbaceous borders
too many times for it to be fun and frolics.

The butterfly whirls between gaping-finger-grasps
Then as nearly always does …this autistic man,
shouts his ear-piercingly loud protestations
he claps at thin blue air changing directions
himself becoming the butterfly, on its maiden flight.
And the butterfly befitting a young, autistic boy
who now thought he too could learn to fly
Somehow pirouettes off on high into the sky.

Mark Andrew Heathcote

Savant

Do you share your world
Or is it yours alone?
Did it evolve with you
Or was it there when you were born?
Within your mystical mind
Was there a seed that grew?
When you emerged into my world
Were you just passing through?
Are you trapped within your mind
Or simply marooned?
Are you harshly imprisoned
Or gently cocooned?
Perhaps you are an Angel
Forbidden the sky,
Or are you just waiting
To learn how to fly?
Am I the one who's lacking?
Are you the one who's whole?
I listen to your music
And know I hear your soul.
Your simplicity is complex,
Your complexity is plain.
My world's loss of you
Becomes your own world's gain.
That you have no purpose
Your Art and Heart belies.
As I watch you fill the canvas
I see the universe in your eyes.

Susan E. Birch

On Autism

Blue is the deep sea
And blue is the sky
Blue are the eyes that charm
And blue, the sapphire we adorn
Blue are the wings of a dancing peacock
But blue is the venom that kills
And blue is the fear that strangles
Blue is the hurt to the little hearts
Whom we don't try to understand
Our indifference and mocking attitude
Make them drown their immense potential

Fatima Afshan

Judo Suits

Job wise learning difficulties
It's not the easiest
It's challenging work, low paid
At times rewarding even fun
Or a paper trail charade.

Caring for one giant of a man
Who'd finish all his sentences?
With the word (then)
Fish & chips (then)
Cup of tea (then) have a bath (then).

Would intimidate many folks
His sheer size and bulk
6ft 2 - his rugged demeanor
New careers looked thunderstruck
Head for the nearest exit-

But to be fair on the whole
He could be a gentle soul.
One thing he didn't tolerate
Were clothes-tags, zips and laces
He'd tear off his own, clothes.

He'd smash up the plates?
And break a few china cups
But he loved a good laugh;
That was all a part of it
How we dealt with his anxieties.

We'd laugh at his improprieties
We'd laugh & share in the joke
In his happier, moments

I Have A Name

But clothes wise in the end:
We had to buy him - judo suits.

Mark Andrew Heathcote

The Question

She asked me, peering into my eyes

"Will my baby ever tell me he loves me?
Will I ever hear those words?"

I struggled for the correct answer for her.

The mysteries of his mind,
for now are locked
The oceans he will swim,
for now are unknown
The secret thoughts,
for now remain his alone

I met her gaze, then the words came.

"Every time he wraps his little arms
around your neck, patting your back;
every time he places his tiny hands
on your face and kisses your mouth,
he has said, I love you, louder, clearer,
than any words could convey; so yes, yes,
he will, you just have to listen harder for
the sound and purity of his sweet voice.

Just listen."

Brenda-Lee Ranta

I Have A Name

Attention Deficit Hyperactivity Disorder

Undiagnosed Disorder

Attention
Deficit
Hyperactivity
Disorder

Say what? Surely not!
you mean me? How can that be
I mean I do not understand my own
psychology or emotional reverie but ADHD?

In hindsight, I now admit the obvious conclusion –
This is no illusion even though it explains my
historical emotional volcanic confusion
I find it hard to follow directions forced to take it
In various sessions – Remembering information
heightens my explosive frustration, cursing and
lexical vomiting my only outlet - Don't even get
me started on organizing tasks, what a pathetic farce
pretending to be in charge!

I find it hard to be on time following the daily social grind
feeling I'm the only one of my kind – Remembering my
childhood isolation even forgetfulness still my adult mental
menace.

Don Beukes

The Misfits Understand

We are the misfits,
The smaller ones, unwanted,
We stay together,
Seeking guidance from the understanding,
The one like us,
We're not popular and might not have friends,
But we know what its like,
To be the underdogs,
We might be small but it's the only way,
We don't know, or choose to be like this,
We have lost some of our own,
To people like you and your names,
Bigger, stronger, smarter? No,
Your words are like glass, cutting us deep,
You throw stones but can't feel this,
The pain, despair, and loneliness,
The anger, shock and feelings for revenge,
Only we, the freaks, losers, the mocked ones,
Have felt this all our lives,
So now I tell you this now,
When it's your turn,
We, are the only ones who understand.

Leigha Beltrame Markon

I Have A Name

What is Normal?

Why must I conform to a standard to
Have a sense of belonging? My brain is capable of
Accomplishing so much, yet I am often cast aside
To someone displaying a more « normal » demeanor.
If my eyes dart from side to side, do you believe that I'm listening?
So lonely I feel, when I'm not understood.
Naturally, I've tried to hide my quirks to
Obtain a sense of normalcy. However, in
Reality, I was denying myself. Was fitting in worth the cost of losing
Myself? The urge for human contact is strong, and it is
Able to tempt me still to silence my busy mind.
Love is a dangerous thing to trade for your life.

Veronique Ginglo-Robert

I Have A Name

Never on the Good Side

When I was young, this doctor gave me pills for ADHD
Then another doctor gave me more pills for OCD
That blasted combination had me so numbed down
I was lost inside myself thinking I would drown

Met a friendly man from the army outside Cheyenne
He promised they would help me become a complete man
Said I could be all I could be and blow up all kinds of shit
I soon learned being a no named screw up just wasn't it

Spent a lot of time angrily caged behind guardhouse bars
Watching brass bring side-chicks in blacked out cars
Alcohol, drugs and whores flowed easy through their night
But grunts get busted for every little thing that wasn't right

Every month the Army's disability check comes in the mail
Still I bust my ass for cash all day hammer and nail
Time spent living a hard life has took away my ADHD
Which the army was kind enough to replace it with PTSD

Now I'm poppin more pills, cause doc says I'm Bi-Polar
In this cracked mirror, seems to me either way I'm a failure
I've lived so long just trying to keep the wolves at bay
Never knowing if today will be my last day

Spending my days watching my troubles get bigger
Spending my nights with my finger on the trigger
I been hiding this damned truth for so long
Searching for a soul lost in the words of every song

Turning up every bottle, I try to mask my dark reality
Always knowing something's different inside of me

I Have A Name

A deep dark swirling mass of unexplainable rage
Unknown by those on the good side of this page

D.B. Hall

The Alphabet Kid

the alphabet kid
what makes you fidget
is the thousand pieces of you
finding solace in solos,
turning fingers into drumsticks
and veins into freeways
traffic-jammed with a chemical crash
where your brain merges into a
never-ending stream of synapses
springing and sliding
pieces gliding and crashing,
head pounding
reality smashing
like your car scraping bark from that tree,
leaves crying on the windshield
spider webbing but not cracking
carrying your perception of okay
to its outer limits
because silence only comes when
the destruction sets in
until then it's this constant onslaught of thought
caught and ripped and tripped,
eclipsing your vision so that
to survive the noise, you explode symphonies
from your skull and
what made you forget
pencils but never the poems,
what looked like apathy
instead of exhaustion
is the same thing that
digs into your skin
while you break out of it;
you breathe in expectation and

I Have A Name

let it burn your lungs
so, you can exhale smoke
because you need
a little blurry when everything is
so freaking sharp that
the clarity cuts your throat
until it bleeds onto guitar strings;
you end up exploding imploding
denoting steps into cymbal crashes,
the frantic frenetic
scurry of that stream that lashes
across your eyelids
and curls under your tongue
is what makes you illuminate
so, radiate through
the alphabet stew they make of you
because what makes you
hard to handle
is also what makes you
brilliant.

Lynne Reeder

ADHD

I still get easily distracted even for a fraction of
a Nano second moment spoiling my mood
constantly misunderstood – I would if I could
listen to you all day but frankly my mind just wanders
as I suddenly imagine future wonders of imaginary
success in a world that shows love less and less unless
if it is in their best interest.

I refuse to take any medication or become a pharmaceutical
human lab rat – I mean what's up with that? As long as
we are loved respected and understood and support one
another – I refuse to submit to adult

Attention
Deficit
Hyperactivity
Disorder

Don Beukes

I Fell in Love with ADHD

In my fragile state I found you,
a lost soul like me.
You helped me learn to laugh and be true
through your ADHD.
We connected so swiftly
and became such good friends
For the first time, I could feel less guilty
and my heart was on the mends.
You didn't care about my space case moments
and I laughed at your care free attitude
I felt like I could fight any opponents,
my brain didn't need a substitute.
You taught me to love my brain,
quirks and all, including the twitching
I never deserved the rejection and pain
and now I feel like I am living.

Veronique Ginglo-Robert

I Have A Name

Schizophrenia

Seroquel Slumber

Heavy doses for the sorrowful~
Deep sleep for Princess Paranoia
Wake early, get in line, swallow~
Psychiatric hospital drill, followed.
Foam cups, plastic food trays~
Watch your back, keep praying
Avoid eye contact and don't dare cry~
Try to close those wide, wild eyes.
Severe depression with psychosis
was the Asian doctor's diagnosis.
Pharmaceutical guinea pig classed~
The idea was to organize these thoughts
but that's like trying to glue smashed glass.
There has to be a righteous remedy
to heal what is eternally broken in me.
It's not found in a bottle or capsule~
I'm better off with ink and a quill.

Christa Frazee

Lunatic Shuffle

Thin mummified
trembling bent fingers
Schizophrenia
resembling razor
sharp raptor talons.
Grasp the burial shovel
with a fervent evil malice.

Reasoned breezes or
teasing chaotic tempests.
Dance on a marshmallow
in a clouded pink fantasy.
Sipping sweet tea with
a lemonade pouted grin.
My jello lunch sucks but a
Thorazine high greets me;
now painting the lawn in
a mixed shaded scheme.

Silver pleated brushes
of bleach blond hair.
Surfing into the fog as
my torch is now hushed.
My friend tried to commit
larceny of my frenzied mind.
I hear his cries for mercy
from the freshly dug grave;
behind the lofty asylum
by the tennis courts where
we loved to sit and watch the
staff relaxing and playing there.

I'm floating over the azure bay

I Have A Name

driving a '57 Chevy Nomad
waltzing into a riotous new decade
whilst in a Prozac lunatic shuffle.

Ken Allan Dronsfield

I Have A Name

The Voices

Insanity, a branch on the family tree,
carved into the heart of you and me
Seeds planted, the day of my arrival,
voices nurtured their tangled survival

Climbed its branches, right to the top,
leaves whisper, talking non-stop
Had no screams, no choices,
the first time I heard the voices

Master minds of heavy metal static,
reciting songs of prayer and panic
Voices on the tongues of whores,
preen in windows, stand in doors

Slipping into a comfy migraine,
inside the screams of pain
Stomach in knots, tied up tight,
voices take me, without a fight

Sanity, forsaken me,
voices, overtaken me
Drown me in doubt
Voices within,
voices without

Alone with the voices,
in my head
Can't hear you,
hear them instead
Millions of maniacs' cry,
you can fly, fly, fly

I Have A Name

Sanity forsakes me
Voices overtake me

I can fly, I can fly, I can...

Hugh Dysart

I Have A Name

Mysylum

There's a padded cell between my ears
A psych ward in my sinner skull
I've been building it for around forty years
I have to keep adding on cause it's always full

Man, there's some crazy stuff in here
like greed and selfishness, lust and fear
They just walk the hall's like no one's near
All kinds of noises like screams, moans and tears

I don't like to sleep cuz that's when they conspire
And awake is the only way I know if they catch fire
Then I can put them out, not let them near that live wire
Hanging loose in the shadows of my mind throbbing with sins desire

I am Mr. Hyde
Whenever I'm inside
But, on the outs I am the door locking Jekyll
In or out doesn't matter, I give me the heckles

They bang on the walls and through the padding, I hear em
End of a long day's curtain call alone, that's when I fear em
They're sleeping on the floor with need of temptations addiction, whispering in empty darkness echoing self-condemnation

I am my own asylum, punch drunk and ready to hurt
Crazy pain my closest companion and a flawless art work
Sometimes with a frying pan, I join them in the corner
In the darkness where I'm unseen, I bang my head a little harder

I Have A Name

I'm paralyzed ya see
By pairs of lies
Or three
And the only one lying to me
Is me
Ya see

There's bars on the inside of these windows
To keep me inside, cause who knows
What kind of hate I could expel all around me
I'm a cross eyed, self-hating, absurdity

The bars on the outside are for your protection
To keep you out of my lack of compassion
I'm boxing with demons but, sparring with angels
Hard to see clearly through my fifty thousand angles

I am stupefied and blown away by myself
The winds of change come sweeping down
I get pushed in and lose the key
And stuck inside my psych ward, I drown

Billy Charles Root

Schizophrenics

When the wiring
of the brain,
unravels in this way like a ball of yarn.
There can be no lonelier
place on earth
than - your own, malicious mind.
Teasing out its, own
self-worthlessness in pain
waging war upon its own self-esteem
its own heart and soul
brother, sister mother father.
And one-time friend and lover
they're all of them voices in your head
but you know you've lost the thread
If, you wish them all dead.

Mark Andrew Heathcote

Head People

She can't recall the day they moved
into her head, so crowded within,
they pushed her out, rearranging
her brain, like interior decorators

Aggressive, pushy, telling her what
to do, they said they were there for
protection; she slept on the floor after
warning her about government plots

Her bed was wired with electrodes that
scan her body, they needed her for the
medical experiments, she must whisper
or they will find her there, hiding away

The ones in her head told her, all the
telephones were trying to suck out her
brains through the earpiece; so, she
pulled all the cords from their jacks!

Her radio was for sending encrypted
messages; she had to stuff cotton balls
into her ears, to block their insidious
transmissions with their secret codes

The government finally sent the police
to bring her to them; she screamed,
bit, kicked; they tied her to a hospital
bed, drugged her and scanned her

She doesn't recall too much after that,
confined to a sterile mint green room,

I Have A Name

her tongue thick and dry, murky mind,
doctors talking to her in hushed tones

She thinks they are gone, the interior
decorators in her head, hearing only
her own voice, very small, confused;
she just can't remember the dream.

Brenda-Lee Ranta

Crude and Hollow

I grow obscene in loneliness
Wound up in myself
Drearily, shuffling
From room to room
I'm skeletal
Entombed, in a white-walled abyss
With a swarm of phobias
Bumbling overhead
And I ache for the plentiful world
Stretched out of my bounds
For I'm far
Too crude and hollow
To be grazed, by the sun's caring rays

William Wright, Jr.

North of Reality

She's just north
Of the border
Of Insanity
Where she's been digging
A little grave
For Reality
She marks the spot
With a mound of mud
And leaves behind a trickle
Of her own heart's blood
There's nothing to grieve for
But her own small life
So, she cuts through
The border of insanity
With her imaginary knife.

C. J. Clark

Downward Spiral

It was totally unexpected, to say the least;
when your happiness was sapped,
and Sadness crept over your countenance.
You were living the life.
Borderless.
Sky was the limit.
A quintessential bachelor
who once wore the diadem of massive success
at a breakneck speed.
I watched you from a distance but closely.
How the yesteryears
carried on a dark plot that twisted your fate.
A juicy canard casting your entire kin;
full of clandestine affairs.
The stigma of a bastard
spread rapidly like a forest fire.
The flames swallowed your every reason to live.
A tattered soul was left
that breathes through the nostrils of shame
and confusion
I missed seeing your auburn eyes;
once beaming with pride.
Now dull with a sickening coldness.
Permeating your entire being.
How your taciturn demeanor
Endears you to the creepy and nocturnal creatures
The moon your regular patron.
You
Pound
Scream
Howl
And fight your
Faceless Foe

I Have A Name

Day after day
Year after year...
In the same spot
Where you chose
To end
Everything

At last.

Carolyn Gutierrez-Abanggan

I Have A Name

I Have A Name

Bipolar ~ Personality Disorders

I Have A Name

Bubbles of Emotion

Honey-colored locks in a ponytail,
She skips along through wind and through hail,
From one colored bubble of emotions to the next.
First to Excitement, a buzz full of flutters
Moving pictures all flashing in bold colors
Flutter bugs that fuzz around inside of you,
While pink fluffy clouds come to obscure your view.
Then onto Euphoria, a room filled with light
Flying round and leaving a glint in your eyes
Where you'd wildly run and jump and skip around.
Listening to your heart pounding up and down.
Later, in the pale violet Bubble of Calm
On a cloudy mattress she lays her head down
And while her forehead is drenched in Misty Spray
The corners of her mouth are pulled up to stay.

"Is it nice back there,
With all those colorful jets?"
A grey, blurry beetle asks.
Her face breaks into a grin
As she eagerly tells him,
All about the room full of bubbles.
"Try it out! It'll solve all your troubles."

The beetle nods and thanks her.
Little does she understand how,
One day,
You are punched
And a hundred strong hands
Push your chest down
And grasp your head
And tiny little things

I Have A Name

Like the chance to commit to what might be worth it,
Ignoring all the pain by tricking your brain
And lying down after a day's work done
Just don't matter in the big, dark uncaring
Void of the universe.

Lilly Moore

I Have a Name (slipping away)

With Furtive glances, they rush by.
I know they see me.
I have a name

Day after day it's the same,
Rushing by in their expensive shoes.
I think they see me.
I have a name.

As each day passes I feel less and less solid,
I'm slipping away.
Maybe they can't see me.
I'm sure I had a name.

And like a bright beacon of light she spoke to me
She saw me, she saw me and smiled.
I have a name.

Dawn Van Leeuwen

Insanity

Sanity has left my head, pouring out from mine eyes in a downpour of dry tear storms and ground pounding of the hoofs of my heart beat as my soul marches on.

The chill of the world wide wicked wind encircles my entire being and my skin retracts pulling tightly against the structure of my core.

My eyes see only night, only dark and only evil. Wicked hearts lying to each other and lying hands are all covered in blood and filth.

Man has gone full mad, for he is enticed, captivated and carried away by hate of fellow man and lust of self, leaving behind the smell of nothingness.

But, my spirit speaks to me in the midst of the clouds and I see the sunset is most beautiful when the sun shines from behind said clouds.

Birth is beautiful in dark of death and death in light of birth, roses bloom after rain from a gray sky and then the sun, while manure covers their roots.

Suddenly the warmth of love engulfs me and my being thaws, skin relaxes and my once dried out pouring tears wet themselves with the moisture of a kiss.

I watch my love sleep in each room where it lies for the night giving my thanks as I look in and supplicate for those who have not.

I Have A Name

And the cycle begins anew as I wake from the night unto a newly given day.

Billy Charles Root

Bipolar Mind

Mania
Exploding with euphoria
I feel as if I can tightrope through the clouds with angels
Feeling invincible
I go shopping for a new dress
Thinking I am invisible, I steal it
This new orange jump suit courtesy of the local jail is not my color
My thoughts and words are racing at an accelerated speed
I am running in place
Going somewhere but never getting anywhere
Devouring a dozen Krispy Kreme doughnuts
Chocolate, cream filled, and sprinkles feel like heaven on my tongue
High on life with the wind in my hair
Speeding down the coast, where I stop nobody knows
Eight hours later finding myself in San Francisco
My life is grand!
Bright like a handful of Skittles
I could slide down a rainbow and land on a cotton candy cloud
I could swim in a milk chocolate lake while drinking a strawberry shake
My life is grand!
Depression
Feeling like I am suffocating
As the devil dances on my chest
Crouching in my shower, paralyzed
Feeling the cold tiles against my buttocks and back
Praying the water will wash away my despair
Guilt consumes me for the pain I have caused others
Feels as if I am sinking in quicksand
Hope it buries me alive if it will take away this shame

I Have A Name

Gorging myself on a dozen Krispy Kreme doughnuts
Chocolate, cream filled, and sprinkles feels like Hell on my tongue
Feeling blue
I walk alone on the beach
Isolating myself from the world
My only companion is the fog as it engulfs me with a hug
Trying to breathe new life into me
I hide in my bedroom in the dark
Hoping no one will hear my cries of pain
My tears feel like acid
Burning as they roll down my cheeks
I am fragile and brittle
I am not anyone's project
I am not Humpty Dumpty for you to put back together again
Healing
I do not let bipolar define who I am
It has been a long road toward getting well
I embrace my disorder, not letting it control me
I find love and gratitude in each waking day

Kelly Klein

Set Me Free

My demons always steal my sleep
Tormenting me through the night
Exhaustion is a heavy cloak to wear
Though weary I cannot quit, I will fight

This anchor weighs upon my chest
There is no end, no reprieve
Even my soul needs some rest
I need that in which I can believe

People never seem to understand
That my mind is always twisted inside
Doctors think the answer is in pills
Two brains in one with nowhere to hide

This has owned me for so damn long
Is this a preview of a hellish destiny?
Someone sing me the Reaper's song
Sing it loud and set me free.

D.B. Hall

The Park of Life

Rough is this walk
where grass is not grass
but jagged glass

Like unsettled spirits
the malevolent picnickers
howl and attack

It's a tightrope walk
holding onto sanity
like a spider its web

making wrong moves
and swallowing
their consequences

a nightly struggle
to not reach for the blade
or the pills
no matter how much
one thinks about it

an attempt to live
without a golden trophy
yet to die with honor
victory flowing in the blood

Jackie Chou

Self-Medicated

your arms,
once curling around a guitar
like grapevines, now
scarred branches broken
by time and
blackness cold as a needle point.

your eyes
that sparked across faces once
searching for hope
have gone
pinprick tight,
stars fading
shadows covering
truths scraping
screaming
tearing through
the tie-off
you couldn't even get to
the sliding in your skull
too gone beyond,
ripping right through your veins
and into
psychiatric restraints,
a winter storm,
cracking and breaking over
syllables tracing the curve of a diagnosis
crystallizing into
all the ways you'll
never be the same.

Lynne Reeder

I Have A Name

White Noise (scream out)

Darkness creeps in, noises scream out
the anger inside begins to shout
Violent temper securely holds
addiction's reality molds

Another crater in the wall
disconnected; makes your skin crawl
Glassy, clouded eyes stare at me
deceived; we are the enemy

Silence the voices of the night
so strung out, not seeing the light
Stay awake, even sleep is brief
in a haze, the only relief

Dragging; the new cycle begins
never-ending sleep; giving in
Days go by, you just don't care
Life; it's just too much to bear

Chattering starts, not making sense
no better, we go on the defense
Ups and downs, no one knows what to do
self-medicating; hinders you

Fast forward ten years, here we are
through broken hands, walls, hearts and cars
The rage simmers, but fear lingers hard
illnesses' wrath leaves all scared

Renee Kline

Manic Kiss

Spiraling through attitudes~
Full-fleshed, eager to believe...

Ready to forgive & embrace
The collective experience…

Tender scar into holy armor.

Still, many hours are still spent
In quick-sand type thinking~

Still, I'm sinking in a sense of
Perpetual ache and incompletion...

My heart is a half-digested riddle.

Maybe I could splatter-paint
The blank paper-white walls?

Or maybe just bedazzle or tie-dye
My sterilized straight-jacket?

This manic mood could
Use a psychedelic kiss of color...

And I brought only my black cloud,
Bible and flaming red riding hood.

Christa Frazee

Psycho

Here comes the girl in black
Known as the "Psycho," others call her "Maniac"
Heading towards the grave she secludes
Herself to her daunting solitude

Beneath her dark glasses enshrouds
Her eyes having lost their glisten
Walking hastily shunning the crowd
Whose eyes hold nothing but scorn and derision

Espy, however, deprived of vision
"Who does she think she is?"
When she's striving to cover the desperation
On each wound and scar on her wrist

She used to be "Normal" by their definition
The time she befriended life
To eventually be a victim of cannibalism

She trusted and loved who didn't hold on
To her, hurled her far upon viciously stepping on

She neither needs friends nor life nor love
She used to long for them, but she's had enough
Here comes the Psycho everyone sees
If she's the Psycho," what should others be?

Mahinour Tawfik

With Love from Bi-Polar in Alaska

There seems to be a battle
In the pathways of my mind
Conflicting information
Past and present enter-twined
Re-tracing every single thought
Can be a tedious task
I sometimes lose the answers
To questions that you ask
One minute I am happy
Then comes the flood of vintage tears
Words said inappropriate
To hide each and every fear
Fuck the phrase "Post Traumatic"
A disorder culture feeds
It takes away my happiness
It takes whatever it might need
So I'm stealing sweet September
Tho death is perched on golden leaves
If I'm lucky next December
I'll get the chance to actually breathe

Lyne Beringer

I Cannot Let the Nightmares Win

I sometimes worry
that I'm annoying
even when
I've been reassured I'm not,
and apologize for things
that are not my fault;
please be patient with me
I am trying
really I am trying even when it seems
as if I am regressing
I try to make progress in improving
myself
so I am not anchored down
to the bottom of the sea of my nightmares
forgotten to everyone including time—
sometimes the monsters scream
louder than the dream,
but I cannot; will not give up because
I have a magic that is only mine
will use my power to improve this world
even if I must simultaneously
improve on myself
because I cannot let the monsters rule
cannot let the nightmares win.

Linda M. Crate

Blissfully Waiting for Lithium's Last Kiss

Heartlessly waiting and regretfully abating
questioning the motif of an abstract work
wishing to feel the tweak or feted treats
as the prick in the arm burns so lovely.
Stand in a street now feeling less bleak
the Count reaches ten, the Muppets dance
the pain is long gone, Miss Piggy looks hot!
June thaw they say, what time is it anyway?
The cop looks scared; stares me in the eyes
he checks my name with his portable radio
asks why I'm on the roof trying to fly, I say,
just blissfully waiting for Lithium's last kiss.

Ken Allan Dronsfield

On Level Ground

Terror on high
Horror on low
Both inside
Know you know
Dying
Crying
Hiding
Lying
When time brings
False hope
Hope brings
False time
Out of rhyme
Cognitive
Distortions
These are the signs
I'm splayed
And layer out
Sprawling
Brawling
Stalling
Calling
Take me up
Take me down
For God's sake
Deliver me
On level ground

John Walker

It's Where I Hide

My world is huge.
Huge describes many troubles.
Troubles keep reason away.
Away my thoughts drift.
Drift in the clouds.
Clouds loom, dark, scary.
Scary eyes judge actions.
Actions are my voice.
Voice escapes, unclear, confusion.
Confusion pushes me inward.
Inward, I am safe.

It's where I hide.

Kathy-Lynn Cross

I Have a Name (it could be anyone's)

I can be manic. Hell, I can be manic as all get out. Sometimes I find myself frozen to my chair, or the side of my bed, unable to instruct my brain on how to perform the simple task of standing up. Sometimes, I am so filled with anxiety, I pace the floor, convinced I might actually be able to escape the skin holding me hostage. And sometimes I am completely consumed with the chaos in my head; as if there might be several versions of me inside, all fighting for control. This is part of who I am.

I'm also intelligent and clever, with an ability to remain calm and focused when it counts; when nobody else seems able. I'm thoughtful, creative, and a semi-emotionally balanced individual. I love with all I have, even when I falter, and I have faltered often.

I struggle mentally with the knowledge that I'm no longer a spring chicken. I will move throughout the days like I always have, ageless and unaffected by the constraints of time. Then I'll catch a glimpse of myself in the mirror, startled by the reflection in front of me. When my weight fluctuates, the mirror and the camera seem intent on showing the worst of me. That's what I believe, regardless of what anybody else might say. This is part of who I am.

I've struggled with addictions. This too, is part of who I am.

But here's the kicker; a silver lining of sorts. I'm still here. I have weathered many perfect storms during my days on Earth. I've earned every single bulge, wrinkle and scar my body carries. It's not a burden, it's an honor to have had the

I Have A Name

privilege of climbing that giant mountain of time and landing here, just on the other side; perhaps wiser, even though fully flawed. Yes, my friends, I'm grateful - totally grateful.

I have a name… It could be anyone's name…

Lyne Beringer

I Have A Name

Epilogue

Publishing Assistance

Starving Artist

In 2013 Ms. Raja Williams realized that there was a gap, a void if you will, within the publishing industry. A writer either had to come up with hundreds, sometimes thousands of dollars to release a book or take on the journey of self-publishing alone. There was no middle ground, no one there to assist, either financially or lead the way in self-publishing. Most writers do not have the finances to pay a publisher, and some don't know where to start when it comes to self-publishing, nor are they prepared to be in business for themselves.

Raja was inspired to start a fund to assist writers in becoming published authors at either a discounted rate or a full publishing scholarship. To begin this fund Raja paid for the publishing of our first anthology Love, a Four Letter Word. Comprised of poets from all around the world. The sales generated from the purchases of the book were placed into a fund that enabled us to fund future publishings.

I Have A Name

We now are able to offer anthology publications, a chance for authors to have a voice in the literary world yearly, and we have been able to offer several authors full scholarships, as well as offering deeply discounted publishing services as a whole. We are thankful for the continued support of this program by both our readers and writers alike.

For More Information Please Visit Our Website At:

www.ctupublishinggroup.com/starving-artist-fund.html

Creative Talents Unleashed

Get Connected With Us!

Website: Creative Talents Unleashed Publishing Group

www.ctupublishinggroup.com

Facebook: Get connected with us on our Facebook Page

www.Facebook.com/Creativetalentsunleashed

Twitter: https://twitter.com/CTUPublishing

Blog: www.creativetalentunleashed.com

Pinterest: https://www.pinterest.com/creativetalents/

Instagram: https://instagram.com/ctupublishinggroup/

Creative Talents Unleashed

Creative Talents Unleashed is an independent publishing group that offers writers an opportunity to share their writing talents with the world. We are committed to fostering and honoring the work of writers of all cultures. Our publishing group offers writing tips to assist writers in continued growth and learning, daily writing prompts and challenges to keep the writers mind sharp and challenged, marketing and events, as well as a variety of yearly publishing opportunities. We are honored to be assisting writers in the journey of becoming published authors.

Creative Talents Unleashed

www.ctupublishinggroup.com

For More Information Contact:

Creativetalentsunleashed@aol.com

www.ingramcontent.com/pod-product-compliance
Lightning Source LLC
Chambersburg PA
CBHW071511040426
42444CB00008B/1601